I0048877

Make Money Work For You

PURSUING FINANCIAL FREEDOM WITHOUT YOUR DAY JOB

BRUCE WALKER

Copyright © 2019 by Bruce Walker

All Rights Reserved

Disclaimer:

No part of this publication may be reproduced or transmitted in any form or by any means, or transmitted electronically without direct written permission in writing from the author.

While all attempts have been made to verify the information provided in this publication, neither the author nor the publisher assumes any responsibility for errors, omissions, or misuse of the subject matter contained in this eBook.

This eBook is for entertainment purposes only, and the views expressed are those of the author alone, and should not be taken as expert instruction. The reader is responsible for their own actions.

Adherence to applicable laws and regulations, including international, federal, state, and local governing professional licensing business practices, advertising, and all other aspects of doing business in the U.S.A, Canada or any other jurisdiction is the sole responsibility of the purchaser or reader.

Content

Introduction

I was talking with a friend not long ago and complained about the legendary "rat race." She laughed at me. Well, to be more accurate, you might say she laughed at my nativity.

What did you expect your work life to be?" she asked, "All fun and games. This is how it is. Get used to it."

Not quite the response I was hoping for. But I wasn't about to let her comments stand. "Didn't you have some Big Dream when you were growing up or even in college? Didn't you envision yourself doing something more with your life?"

Then she gave me the standard, "You have to put your time in at the bottom of a corporation before you can get promoted lecture. "You'll see, she said, "one day you'll realize all this rat racing around was worth it."

That was my moment of realization. The rat race wasn't like the New York City Marathon. You didn't run your heart out and then get a medal for placing. Even if it were somewhere in the middle of the pack.

What is the rat race?

You're probably knee-deep in it already, if you're spending your days at work hating your job, wishing for a more fulfilling career and dreaming of the moment you can turn your office computer off and go home for the weekend.

The rat race is the struggle that many of us feel when we are working at jobs we hate and getting neither self-satisfaction from them nor praise from your supervisors.

And what do you do once you get home on weeknights and weekends?

Answer honestly. If you're like most people you'd confess, "Not much of anything, truthfully." During the week, it takes all the energy you have to get yourself through the commute home, make dinner, and then plop yourself in front of the television to watch some mindless situation comedy program or Netflix movie. And don't even think about reading a good book, because the book will drop to the floor and you'll be sitting there sleeping.

The Rat Race Has No Finish Line

The rat race takes place on one of those wheels you see in hamster cages. You jump on the wheel and run your heart out only to discover that you're going nowhere. And the faster you run and harder you try . . . well, the faster you're getting to nowhere.

I only see myself – and everyone else I know – living painfully from paycheck to paycheck from one weekend to the next fully resigned to cling to jobs they hate, bosses that don't respect them and home lives that aren't much more exciting than sitting on the couch waiting for the next program or movie to come on.

No, what I'm talking about is a desire to make a clean break from the rat race and do something I love doing. I would love to make money on my terms. I would love nothing better to go on vacation when the mood hits me and to stay for as long I want. With no email from the office following me, no urgent texts that need attention, no fires to put out at work.

Yes, now you're getting the big picture of exactly what I want – financial freedom. Don't get me wrong, I'm not looking for the winning lottery tickets. I'm more than willing to work for financial freedom. I'm eager in fact, to tackle something I love and make enough money to live on it and to invest it so eventually, I can do just that.

The more I thought about this possibility, the more fascinated I became by it. And so, I began to do two things. First, I gave serious consideration to what I would do to make the ultimate living. What I wanted was a job that didn't feel like a job.

I started researching how I would go about ensuring that if I decided to march into my boss's office today and told him to shove . . . I mean to politely inform him I was resigning, how much money I would need to keep me living until my Big Dream began earning me money.

I didn't tell anyone at first. I refused to disclose my Big Dream for fear people would laugh at me or worse yet try to talk me out of it. Then at the same time, I began to research if it were feasible to leave the rat race, exiting by a side road.

What I discovered shocked and surprised me. But most of all, it sent an electrical charge of hope through me. What I wanted to do could pay off financially – and with an income much nicer than my current job.

The kicker? I had to save enough money to be able to put some cash away as a cushion in case I ran into a slow period or two. Since I was living paycheck to paycheck I took a deep breath to see if this were possible. After all, the statistics tell us that the average family, the average employee was only one paycheck away from bankruptcy.

Now that's not the news I wanted to hear, but it was news I needed to hear. So I began to investigate how to bump up my income, invest my money and begin living my Big Dream.

What about you?

Are you tired of the rat race? Have you begun to think of your Big Dream – starting your own business, writing a novel, going back and re-learning how to play your high school musical instrument or maybe reviving that acting "career" with the community theater – and beyond?

Here are just a few symptoms and signs that indicate you may be ready to start preparing yourself for making a leap of faith – off of the rat race wheel and into your own version of paradise.

Symptom #1: You hate your job

Well, at the very least it doesn't bring you the enjoyment it once did. Think back to when you were offered that position. There must have been a reason or two you accepted it? Think about how you felt when your supervisor gave it to you.

What happened? Why can't you bring back the same feeling of satisfaction to your work, even dare I say eagerness?

If you can't, you may be ready to quit the rat race.

Symptom #2: You're not feeling as physically healthy as you once were.

Oh, there's not one thing you can point to that makes you feel less than physically fit. You may be thinking all along you just need to take some vitamins, get a bit more exercise into your day or improve your diet. Or then again, years of racing on a wheel may be taking a physical toll on your body.

Symptom #3: You can't find time for you.

Ever feel as if your day is being orchestrated and decided by those around you and you have little say in its direction? This is a good indication that you may be ready to call the rat race quits.

Half of the deadlines you're facing at work at nearly impossible to meet. And the other half? They were all due yesterday. What's worse, you can't see the end of it. There's no way you can even hope to get caught up.

Symptom #4: You're beginning to worry about losing your job.

No, you can't' pinpoint exactly why you feel like this, which only fuels your anxiety all the more. All you know is that you stopped giving 100 percent to your work several years ago. And you're sure "they" will discover the deception any time now.

Symptom #5: You're becoming increasingly irritated with every aspect that occurs in your life.

You never felt road rage before, but that "jerk" that just pulled out in front of you made you awfully made. The guy at work, the one in the office next door, is also beginning to get on your nerves. Funny, you never noticed he was so irritating before.

Or is he?

Could it be the way you react to your co-worker and the other driver? You've encountered people like this for a long time now and ever felt like that before. So why now? What's the difference?

Yes, it could very well be your view of your job and your increasing dissatisfaction and growing stress with the rat race.

Symptom #6: You know you're good at your job, but you're not getting the promotions.

Instead, others who have been with your company a shorter period of time and have less experience than you are getting promoted. And you sit there in the same office getting passed over. You know in your heart you would be better than they in that newly opened job. All you need is the opportunity to show them. Why can't they see that?

CHAPTER 1:

~

Don't Follow the Rat

So you don't want to follow the rat in front of you. You'd like to break out of the pack and head off on a path all your own.

Personally, I know where you're coming from. Probably the signature symptom that it was time for me to think about doing something – anything – different from my life was the ennui that set in anytime I thought about my job.

I didn't want to live my life being tired anymore. I needed more of a reason to wake up during the week than the latte at the nearest Starbucks. I needed to live on purpose.

You may think that all your neighbors and friends have this same driving desire to do something more with their lives – to make a mark somewhere, anywhere other than their drab office and a boring job.

You'll be surprised that when you casually mention your dream, how many people will try to talk you out of it. They'll try to convince you that you *need* this job. I heard a conversation once between a dissatisfied frustrated waitress at a coffee shop once expressing her displeasure with her colleague about not only the job but her supervisor as well.

She was on the verge of quitting, right there. Until, that is her friend told her, "You can't quit, you need this job." I wanted to jump up and tell you, "Not if you're going to be humiliated by customers and your supervisor alike. You can find another job where you'll be treated better."

She didn't leave because she wasn't sure she could find anything better. Perhaps for her staying there was the right move. I saw more than just her quitting, I saw into the future and finding the right and perfect job— or better yet – home-based business or online enterprise that could bring in just as much if not more. But people told her she shouldn't do it.

Another gentleman I knew got laid off from his warehouse job. Instead of worrying about where his next substantial paycheck was coming from, he worked online while he was laid off. He had already started a small Kindle publishing company. Now he thought would be the perfect time to make it work full time for himself.

And several months when the warehouse called him back to work, he said thanks, but no thanks. He was making more money with his own business than he was at his former 40-hour workweek at the warehouse.

Then they'll be those individuals that will tell you escaping the rat race is a bad idea. "What if your business doesn't take off? What will you do?"

Or those who caution you that if you must do, then you need a "back up" plan. That way if it doesn't work, you have a cushion to land on.

Ignore these people and don't allow them to drag you back into the rat race. They may be okay with the same old grind, the same office, the same routine. But clearly, you hear something different calling you.

Why are they trying to keep you in your hamster wheel running the rat race?

A handful of these people truly believe that unless you have the right contacts and the money already, there's no way in this day and age to make money outside of a nine to five job. They are sincerely fearful you may fail. At least if you stay in the rat race, you do have a "next" paycheck to look forward to as meager at it seems.

Their message is loud and clear: it's better to deal with what you're familiar with than venture into the unknown.

Then there are those individuals who may actually be jealous of your decision. They may have had a Big Dream of leaving the rat race behind and living life on their own terms at one time. They may have had an idea for a business, but couldn't or wouldn't leave, not only the comfort of their surroundings but the safety and security of a regular paycheck.

Whatever the reasons, the moment you make your move, you'll discover people who are ready to jump up and judge you. Some are rooting for you to make it. Just realize others are waiting for you to re-enter the race, so they can tell you, "I told you so."

Delayed Gratification

If there were a way to start a business and at the same time enjoy everything material life has to offer you, no one has yet found the secret. The truth of the matter is that if you're in the rat race living paycheck to paycheck, something has to change if you're going to be successful in achieving your financial freedom.

And that's exactly why the vast majority of those employed now will even consider entrepreneurship let alone actually make the giant leap you're considering right now. They have grown far too accustomed, you might even say dependent, on a regular paycheck. Take even one away from them and their finances would crumble around them.

While you may be well aware of the need for giving up the purchase of that set of golf clubs in order to eventually invest it in your business. Or you may have your eyes on that gorgeous pay of red heels that you'll never buy because you've squirreled money away towards the needs of your startup.

Your business –eventual financial freedom – is far more appealing, and comforting than any shoes or set of a golf club can ever be.

But the crucial concept to keep in mind, some individuals either forget or never knew, is that for the first few years of your business at least, you'll still be making these types of judgments.

When a few profits roll in they believe they owe it to themselves to celebrate and reward themselves by buying something. Which is fine. What many individuals don't do is reinvest their profits in their business to ensure the extended growth of their business.

The Parable of the Two Trees

It's like what I call "the parable of the two trees." No you probably won't find this parable quoted in any scripture, but if you study nature, you cannot but be struck by the lesson nature teaches you with this if you're willing to listen.

China has a tree called the Moso Bamboo. This tree has an amazing growth rate at the first several years of its existence. It is remarkable because of its "choice" of growth. The first several years of its life, it's growing by leaps and bounds. But if you were to look at where it was "planted" you'd find no evidence of this. That's because the growth is taking place beneath the surface of the earth. It's busy growing and forming an extensive root system.

It's only after the Moso Bamboo has dug its roots into the ground deeply and securely will it begin to sprout any stem or leaves above the surface. During these years, it appears to the casual observer that nothing is happening. If you didn't know about the way this tree grows, you'd think the seeds didn't take.

And when the Moso Bamboo does grow, it does so at an amazingly fast rate. Some say it may only take it less than a year for it to grow eighty feet, thanks to its superior and efficient root system.

In contrast, let's talk about the Cottonwood Aspen. It grows every bit as tall as the Moso Bamboo and it too does so at a breakneck speed. It will match the eighty-foot bamboo foot-for-foot. But unlike the Moso Bamboo, the Aspen has failed to create a nearly impenetrable root system.

What does that mean? It means that a strong wind could knock it down, a wind that wouldn't even begin to threaten the Moso Bamboo.

As you work your way to financial freedom, keep this parable in mind and always ask yourself: am I the bamboo or the Aspen?

This is an excellent story whenever you begin to doubt yourself or begin to question the time and investment you're spending at your business. You're busy taking the path you've chosen because you're highly aware of the value of money, time and expertise at investing in both.

One last thought

Remember, that as you create your own path toward a new life and financial freedom, you'll always have critics. You'll have enough people to judge you. Some of these people you know; others you won't know. But all of these individuals will be more than happy to take swings at you. You're making money and breaking away from the pack.

But you'll learn how to ignore them all and allow all their remarks to simply bounce off you.

"Entrepreneurship is living a few years of your life like most people won't, so that you can spend the rest of your life like most people can't."

CHAPTER 2:

~

Knowing Where You Are in Life

Have you ever heard someone, in jest say, you can't get there from here?

Do you feel like that's the truth about your journey to financial freedom? You look at where are at this moment and then look way up the path of financial freedom and you can't see any way you could possibly get there from where you presently are?

The truth of the matter more people than you'll ever know have stood exactly in the same spot you have and have achieved financial freedom. People have stood farther away from the financial freedom sign and have made it.

It doesn't matter how money – or how little money – you have at the moment. It doesn't matter how old you are, whether married, singled, or widowed. And certainly, your current financial status won't block you from getting to the point of financial freedom and out of the daily rat race.

There are two keys to getting yourself to your vision of financial freedom. The first key is to know where it is you want to go. And then the second key is being aware of where you are now.

Think about how the GPS in your car or your phone works. The only two things either of these devices want to know your current address and the address of your destination. That's it. Any other information you give your GPS is only going to confuse it. You'll have it "recalculating" until its battery dies if you're not careful.

The key to getting there is just being aware of your current financial status – without judging it. Just accept it and make plans for success.

Don't keep your eyes on the others breaking out of the mold or those who decide to run the rat race. Instead, keep your eye on what you want and how you plan on getting there.

Set your intention, plan your trip and then go.

If you want to get there from here, then there are two aspects of your life you should begin to examine and ponder as soon as possible. The faster you can get these two concepts clearly posted in your mind, the faster the trip to financial freedom will be.

The first is where is it you want to go. In order words, 'What's your dream?" Is it to own your own business, either online or brick and mortar? Is it supporting yourself and having money left over through writing fiction?

You may want to retire early. Why? What would you do with your extra years of retirement?

There are no right or wrong answers to any of these questions, just answers that resonate with you.

It very well could be you have something completely different in mind as your dream. Before you take another step toward your dropping out of the rat race, you need to know what it is.

And I don't mean just some idea, I mean a concrete description of what your dream looks like. It needs to be so realistic in your own mind that if it's spending your days at your dream home along the beach you feel the salty seawater between your toes.

Your dreams need to be firmly entrenched in your mind so that you can not only see it, but feel it, and taste it.

So what's your big dream? How do you want your life want to look, five, ten perhaps even twenty years from now?

Most of us, move along, without the capacity of even thinking a year ahead of time, let along five or ten years into the future.

Determining Your Big Dream

It's okay while you're deciding on your Big Dream that you write some of these ideas down. In fact, I highly encourage it. Approach it like a brainstorming session or a mind-mapping exercise.

The best question you could ask yourself, in fact, is this one: If money weren't a consideration, what would you do with your time, energy and other resources. Write down all the possible answers that come to mind. Don't limit them.

Once you have all of these options laid out in front of you, don't choose – at least not yet. Keep all of your options open, because it very well be, through the "magic" of financial freedom and the shrugging off of the rat race, that you'll be able to do it all.

In fact, what you might want to do is write them all out. Set them in locations throughout the house where you can read them on a regular basis. As wild, fantastic and perhaps even impossible as some of these dreams may seem to you now, don't judge them. Just continue presenting them to your subconscious mind. Talk to yourself daily about them.

And, here's something you haven't heard since you were a child, it's more than okay to daydream about them. To imagine yourself actually doing these things, acting in these ways.

One more word about setting your intention

If you believe that you're done setting your intention of getting from where you are today financially to where you'd like to be, you're wrong.

Let me suggest one more concept, one more activity. Make a vision board. That's right! I realize to some of you the idea may seem foolish, others of you may not even know what one is.

A vision board is simply a bulletin board or a poster board. On this, you'll place photos, pix and other graphics and sayings about your dreams or your Big Dream. If it's a house on the beach, find a photo of one that appeals to your sensations paste it on the board.

Is it the idea of spending your "retirement years" writing fiction? Find photos conducive to that. Or create a book cover to paste on your board, with your name as author on it. There really are no rules to this.

Know Your Strengths and Weaknesses.

Now that you know where you want to go, you need to take a solid look at your finances right now, so you can analyze where you are right now financially.

For many of us, this is the ultimate "scary" part of the process. It's almost as if we go around not knowing our present status, let alone giving an honest look at our money managing strengths and weaknesses, we think any financial problems we have now will disappear on its own.

They won't. But your procrastination of giving a good, solid --and might I add --nonjudgmental look at them will make all the difference in the world.

Take a good look at the income you have and what's going out every month. Not only that, but check out what you spend it on (in the next chapter, we'll do a more detailed analysis. Right now, you just want to get an overview so you can begin to determine what changes you may need to make in your lifestyle and spending habits.

For example, a young woman with dreams of entrepreneurship may discover the quickest way to reduce her expenses is by going back and living with her parents. If they can negotiate a monthly rent payment that is less than what she currently pays, the temporary inconvenience will be more than worth it.

Some individuals may want to downsize from their current home to a smaller, less expensive one. In this way, they can slash a certain amount of money from their income quickly and put that money toward their goal of financial freedom.

There's yet another group of people who have diligently saved and can actually use a portion of their savings to finance their dream. The only thing holding them back at this point is the mindset that would reduce their savings account.

Of course, they use only a portion of their savings to get started which could be a giant leap for them. They might consider in this arrangement is writing themselves an "IOU." The idea of this is that when they begin to make money, they'll put a certain amount of their profit back into the savings.

Don't make any rash changes at this point. Merely begin to ponder your options. If you want, do the same thing with these options that you did with your dream options. Write them on a piece of paper and think about them a bit.

You may very well be impatient about stepping out of the rat race and beginning your journey toward financial freedom. But this is far too large a step in your life to simply rush into it on a wing and a prayer.

No, you need to lay a solid foundation, much like that Moso Bamboo tree does, growing underground before you even get a glimpse of its leaves. Of course, you want a Big Dream that will stand the winds of storms. A dream and a plan that won't collapse and crumble even when the worst of economic conditions hit.

You're maybe seriously thinking about dropping out of the rat race. In fact, you may have already completed the preliminary work. You have a good idea of how you're going to start your journey of achieving financial freedom.

Of course, you realize at this point, that it just doesn't happen overnight. Few of us have that rich uncle we never met who, nonetheless, leaves us his fortune. No, if we're going to retire early or follow our Big Dream, then we have to be the ones to make it happen.

Many individuals say they've tried to leave the rat race to gain financial freedom several times, but it didn't seem to be in the cards for them. So, they just resigned themselves that they were either more suited to the rat race or destined to be a rat race marathoner.

CHAPTER 3:

❧

Killing Two Birds with One Stone:

The Key to Financial Freedom

As we've discussed, you can't just jump off your hamster wheel one day and say you're abandoning the race. No, as you see, it's an event that you must plan for. If you don't, it's more than likely you're going to be back running the race before you can even catch your breath.

In addition to the work you've done discovering your Big Dream and your related blueprint for building a foundation of financial freedom there's still in vital achievement you have to conquer.

You have to be able to eliminate bad habits from your life and replace them with good habits. In other words, you'll have to assess the habits you'll need to change or add to your life in order to get you to your goal.

The more good habits you have – those things you do throughout the day without even thinking about it – the easier you'll find your journey. It'll also be easy to keep your finances. Your good habits will also mean that it'll be much easier to make smart choices that you won't regret, choices in fact that propel you on the road to your Big Dream.

What kind of habits and choices do I mean? There's an adage about killing two birds with one stone. Thankfully, it really has nothing to do with actually killing birds. It's more about making choices and establishing habits that will not only favorable affect you here and now, but to help you as you work on manifesting your goals.

It's making a choice that is referred to as a win-win situation. That means that it not only provides you with an advantage at the time you make your choice, but it provides you with advantages for your achieving your goal.

Let's take a quick look at just one example to start. Let's say that you want to lose weight. So you decide to take a bit of your savings or place a purchase on your credit card for a treadmill. Now, let's also say you also use it regularly.

This decision to purchase the treadmill can easily be seen as a "win-win" choice. First, it provides you with short-term benefits in keeping your weight down and eventually losing weight. Beyond that, though, losing weight will not only boost your energy level, but help improve your productivity and in the long run, could very well be a crucial aspect of your having the energy and mindset to achieving your goal of financial freedom. And just as an aside, it may also help you with that expensive gym membership you talked yourself into buying last January.

Just as there are choices that are characterized as "win-win," there are decisions and habits that can only be labeled as "lose-lose." Let's take the example of my neighbor, who wants to unchain himself from his nine-to-five job. He's making plans, but he complains there just don't have enough time in a day to do everything he wants to.

Last week he knocked at my door and asked if I would help him carry in a new purchase he made. I was thinking it was probably a new desk that he could dedicate to making his preliminary plans for his goals.

Instead, I found myself helping him carry in a large – extremely large—television. We hooked it up and I left quickly before I let my true feelings known.

There are many situations when a purchase like that is a great action. But, if your goal is to create a path to your financial then, then a large, expensive television might be the perfect illustration of a "lose-lose" choice.

First, he's diverting money that could be eventually used toward furthering his goals and buying something that will only drain more time from his goal-making plans. That three to four hours in the evening he had free when he came home from work is now going to be preoccupied watching television on that awesome large screen.

This purchase is a "lose-lose" choice. First, my neighbor has taken money away that could have been used to further his goals. Secondly, he immediately filled up the time he did have after work with watching television. He, now, less time than ever, given his choices and priorities to further his dreams.

Another example of a "lose-lose" choice is my co-worker who eats his lunch nearly every workday at McDonald's. There are plenty of healthy choices these days at this fast-food restaurant. But he chooses, instead, greasy hamburgers, large orders of deep-fried French fries and mind-numbing sugar-laden soda. Then he wonders why the rest of the day, his mind seems foggy and he can't seem to get his energy level back.

The following is a list of six techniques that will help you make more "win-win" choices on your road to financial freedom and ensure that the good choices you've made up to know become long-term healthy habits – activities you do that natural advance your financial goals without your even thinking twice about implementing them.

Habit-forming Technique #1: Be crystal clear in knowing what activity you want to develop into a habit.

You should not only know what the habit you want to know is, but why it's important to your long-term goals. For example, let's say you're wading into social media for the first time regarding your dream. Don't just tell yourself that your goal is to be "more visible" in social media.

Can you see where that is a vague statement? What type of social media, Facebook, LinkedIn, Twitter? Let's say you've been told that you could easily begin to market your business on Facebook with amazing results.

Then the way to do this is to say, "I am learning how to use Facebook to market my widget." The more specific you can be the better. Then your first step is to learn everything you can about how it works and how Facebook can work in getting you closer to achieving your Big Dream.

Habit-forming technique #2: Schedule it into your routine daily.

That's right. There's no use in creating that goal, then allowing it to slip through the cracks. Work on this topic even ten minutes daily. In this way, you keep this goal uppermost in your conscious mind. Make it an appointment with yourself that you can't skip – like an appointment with one of your clients at work.

How do you schedule it? Treat it just like any other important meeting. Would it help you to remember taking time out for your Facebook appointment is you wrote it down in your planner? Then do it. You may want to set a daily alarm on your cell phone that is clearly identified as your Facebook learning time.

Don't become self-conscious if this is the only step you're taking toward developing a long-term habit. Instead, congratulate yourself on learning about it and eventually using it. Make sure you make it a time when you feel comfortable doing this. Don't just stick this "appointment" with Facebook in someplace where you feel rushed.

Habit-forming Technique #3: Monitor your new habit.

Nothing succeeds like success. And nothing feels better than building a momentum toward that success. That's exactly why you should monitor your new-found habit. To make your new Facebook activity a habit, something you do, not out of thought, but almost reflexes, you'll have to keep track of your actions. This is a crucial step, especially in the early stages of sealing it in your subconscious.

The obvious action to take then would be to track how often you're on Facebook and to track at least loosely how many are visiting you on the social media giant. Human nature is funny in a way, the more you do something, the more you want to do something.

That goes for everything we do. When I bought a used car nearly a decade ago, I decided just for fun to keep track of my payments. The more I could pay towards the car, the more excited I was to pay it off.

Tracking your time and responses on Facebook is not only a way to create a habit But to start your business as well as the first of many new, good habits, you're forming as you learn the ropes of your new venture.

But, here's the best part. Take a look at what this exercise in forming a new good habit produces. It's a win for you because you've learned a new skill or have become adept at this activity.

But it's another sense it's a win because you now have a better grasp of your marketing strategy that can help you grow your business.

It is, without a doubt, that "win-win" situation we talked about earlier in the chapter.

CHAPTER 4:

~

Calculating Where You Stand Financially

You feel prepared to start your business, head off in the direction of your Big Dream, and especially dropping out of the rat race.

It's great that you're enthusiastic about your new endeavor, but you're not quite finished preparing for what should be the tipping point of your life. You still need to do possibly the most important preparatory steps in your plans.

Defining your monthly expenses

It's difficult to make coherent financial goals or consistent steps toward financial freedom if you don't know how much money you spend every month. Earlier in the book, we talked about knowing how much you make a month. Now you'll get a good, perhaps even painful look to see where you spend that money each month.

If you keep even a modicum of awareness around your money you already have a rough idea. Yet, even those individuals who think they keep meticulous records of their spending, often find something they've forgotten to include.

Tracking your expenses will help you spend your money more wisely.

Between your monthly bills, daily necessities, and the little things you buy along the way, it can be difficult to know where all your money goes. If more cash seems to be going out than coming in, a great way to get control is to set aside some time to calculate your expenses.

If you take the process step-by-step, it can be surprisingly easy to find out how you're spending your money. That's what this chapter is all about. Lying out your expenditures so you can better assess how much you potentially have to set aside for your financial freedom.

Don't get disappointed and definitely don't toss your dream aside, if you find at this moment your expenses may be more than what you earn in a month. The idea isn't to toss your **Big Dream**, but to clear the way to get you started on it.

After performing this examination, many entrepreneurs found that they had to do a lot of saving and yes in some cases sacrificing in order to initially scrape up enough money that would allow them to start

More than one online millionaire tells their readers that before they were making unbelievable sums of money and found their financial freedom that they were living in their cars. They didn't even have enough money to rent an apartment. When you pull together all the numbers that go into your monthly expenses, don't judge yourself, or berate yourself and don't do anything rash like give up before you even gave yourself a fair start.

Just go through these objectively and as impartially as possible.

You'll want to undertake this project when you can spend at least an hour or more on this activity. This ensures that you haven't rushed through it and you've included everything.

Gather your financial statements together

What type of documents are considered financial statements? All of your monthly bills – your utility bills, your monthly memberships to the gym, Amazon prime, and any automatic deductions you may have coming out of your checking account Don't forget either your lease or your mortgage statement.

If you have one or more car payment include these financial statements as well. This gives you a highlight of the largest of your expenses, but you know you're not quite finished yet.

Now you have gathered all of your unvarying monthly expenses. These stay the same every month and are in some cases, unnegotiable (read on as you'll discover ways you can even lower these with some out-of-the-box thinking.)

Create a list of other miscellaneous monthly expenses.

The expenses that don't fall into the proportions of house or car payments or rent. And for the moment, we're going to identify them as being miscellaneous expenses. Later in the chapter, we'll categorize them again. But right now, we're just concerned about gathering all the expenses in one place.

But they're expenses you need to live on. You'll want to start with the most important ones. Think of groceries, clothing (especially if you have a job in retail), haircuts for you and your family (these can get quite expensive when you begin to add them up) gas for your cars,

If you go to the laundromat then estimate how much you spend on one trip and how many trips a month you go in order to get an idea of that expense.

Are you a frequent customer at Starbucks, Dunking Donuts on your way to work? If you stop at a sit-down restaurant on a regular basis estimate how much you spend. If you're not sure what "regular basis" means, you're a regular if the servers are calling you by your first name or know exactly what you're going to order every morning.

For many individuals and families alike, prescription drugs are a big monthly expense. Even if they're a small expense, if you need them on a monthly basis, then include them. Are you taking vitamins or any herbal supplements? These are expenses as well and need to be calculated into your monthly expense sheet.

To help you organize your spending into something a bit more manageable, you may want to divide them into three separate categories: fixed, flexible and discretionary.

Fixed expenses are just what they say. They're the spending that remains the same every month that is vital to your routine. If you've already guessed them you're probably right, rent or mortgage, car payments, health insurance if not taken out of your paycheck, car insurance.

This represents the bare minimum of spending to keep your head above financial waters every month. They are, however, not your only expenses.

Can you reduce these expenses?

You can but these are among the most difficult to reduce, as you might imagine. But, depending on your situation and the intensity of your desire for your goal of financial freedom.

You may decide you want to downsize your home, depending on where your family life is. It could be something you've been thinking about if your children are growing older and at least one has already left for college or is out on her own. Of course, you'd offer to pay rent but what you'd pay your parents probably would be less than what you're currently paying your landlord. This may be an inconvenience for a while but it is an option.

Perhaps your parents are older, though, and your presence with them may be actually a blessing to them and provide you with peace of mind.

Another area in which you want to decrease your expenses is your car payment. Before you think you need to ditch your car altogether, which ultimately you may decide you want to do, consider other options.

Your decision should be weighed first and foremost on how old your car is and the condition of your car from a mechanical point of view. I've driven some cars as long as I could because I dreaded adding another monthly payment to my expenses. If you're doing that now, then you know exactly what I mean.

But there will come a time where the string of repairs you must make on your car at the most financially inopportune times, far exceeds the expense of a monthly payment that you can schedule and plan for.

On the other end of that argument is the person who earns minimum wage who drives a Corvette or another type of expensive sports car. You've got to wonder if he has any money left for anything else in his life once he makes his monthly payment -- and his car insurance payment.

There's the kicker in this decision, as well. The insurance payment. It could be that you could afford a car payment and still be able to tuck money away for your Big Dream. But, the more expensive the car and the more "sporty" it is, the more you'll end up paying in car insurance.

When you consider paying for your car, think about both payments as one before you make your decision

Similarly, if you drive a modest car that gets the job done – gets you from point A to point B without a car payment or a lowered car payment – think about how much the insurance will cost for owning it.

But, if you live in an area, like New York City, for example, where public transportation is reliable and traffic is horrific, think about whether you really need to own a car.

Flexible expenses

The next category is your **flexible expenses**. These are as important to your living from day to day, but they tend to increase or decrease from month to month. What type of expenses would you put in this category?

Start with your utility bills. You may have been tempted to place these in the fixed expenses, they in a real sense aren't. These are the bills you have at least some leeway in the size of the bill.

For example, if your cable bill is a problem, try reducing some of the channels you receive. To be honest, few of us really watch all of the channels included in these packages. Which ones? That depends on the viewing tastes of you and your family.

You'd also be surprised at how just a small adjustment of your thermostat can lower your heating and air conditioning bills. Even just a point or two can make a noticeable impact on your monthly bills.

Discretionary expenses are those that aren't necessary for your survival, but make your life that much sweeter. Many individuals, when they're adjusting their budgets to create room for their financial freedom are far too harsh in this area.

Just as you don't need to eat breakfast out every morning or even stop for coffee (buy a thermal to-go cup and make coffee at home in the morning)., you do need to save some spending "just for kicks."

An occasional latte or an occasional breakfast is fine. Dinner out with your spouse now and then is also necessary. If you carve out a too Spartan of a lifestyle, you'll never be able to stick with it. You'll feel locked into a bargain you really didn't agree to.

Tips for decreased spending priority

In general, you'll want to eliminate or at least lessen the items on which you're paying the most interest. Overall, that might be your mortgage and your car. But if you have any credit cards you use on a regular basis, consider getting this spending under control as quickly as possible.

Whenever possible, the goal is to eliminate as many of these as possible, starting with the ones with the highest interest. You'll be surprised how quickly and how much you can actually save toward your nest egg to walking away from the rat race.

What happens if you do everything within your power to decrease your spending and you still don't think that's going to provide you with enough money to get that dream of financial freedom started?

That's when you turn to your income and you decide how you can increase the amount of money you bring in on a monthly basis. That's exactly what we'll cover in the next chapter.

CHAPTER 5:

~

Generating Assets For The Freedom

If you've thought of all the ways you can reduce your expenses and you still aren't convinced that this will provide you enough money to get you to financial freedom, there's only one option left. And has nothing to do with staying in the rat race.

No, that means, you need to generate a bigger income. I know you are sighing right now. "That's easier said than done," you say.

It might be in some cases, but in other instances, you'd be surprised how easily you can get started earning extra income. Many individuals have been told forever that investing in the stock market and retirement funds will provide them with the best road to eventually financial freedom. The keyword in the previous sentence is eventually.

Your goal, of course, is to step off that hamster wheel as quickly as possible. That means some of the more moderate, less risky ways of investing money aren't exactly what you're looking for. A 401k, for example, is not a quick road to financial freedom, neither is any kind of investing in stocks and bonds.

You'd have a much faster return on your investment if you invested in a business. Now, that sounds a bit more realistic. I know a gentleman who opened his own coffee shop thinking that from the moment it opened he would be making a great income.

He was wrong. Even after four years of being open, he complained he still wasn't breaking even in his venture. What you're looking for is a way to create money in the quickest way possible.

If you research this on the web, you'll get a wide variety of jobs that sound great at first but aren't really worth your time or energy. Many people are now choosing to drive for Uber or Lyft or some other "taxi" like firm. That's always a possibility, but to make the most money you'll have to be available at the most inconvenient portions of the day.

Many people search for an Uber driver after a night of ribald merriment – in other words, heavy drinking. Depending on where you live that would require you to be driving at hours close to two in the morning. Or some call an Uber driver when they need an early morning ride to an airport. Again, not the most wonderful time to work, unless that is you're an insomniac.

In the spirit of helping you find the most lucrative incomes that will quickly generate a noticeable difference in your bottom line, here are just a few you should be wary of. These have been proven time and again, to be not worth your time and energy.

Filling out surveys

At first, glance, getting paid to fill out surveys and surf the web sounds like a great passive income. Activities that you could easily squeeze between your main income and your home life. Besides, everyone surfs the web nearly every day anyway.

But when you scratch the surface of this line of income, you'll discover that it really isn't what it's advertised to be. It's not a difficult work, that's for sure, and it's easy to sign up and get moving. But there a few holes in the details.

Among the many disadvantages is that you can't possibly make enough money to make it worth the time you've invested in it. You make merely pennies a survey and most sites won't even pay you until you've earned twenty dollars. That can take forever.

Investment opportunities

The days of making a fortune as a day trader are over (if they ever really existed) as well as the opportunity to earn money as a foreign currency trading. You may want to think twice before you jump into this type of side job. It's highly unusual to make a great deal of money with either of these examples. Not only that, but the odds are even higher than you'll end up losing money.

I'm sure you've heard that some individuals have made a fortune – in fact, this was their golden ticket out of the rat race and into financial freedom. But the reason for that is due to a quirky combination of hitting one lucky investment and to have the money on hand to invest a large amount at one time.

While that "large amount" of money is what you're searching for the odds aren't in your favor.

What about scrap metal?

Recycling scrap metal, may at first, sound like a great idea. But the problem with this is that the days of scrap yards paying good money are long gone. If you're old enough, you may remember gathering all the soda cans and hauling them to the scrapyard where they start counting out what seemed like an inordinate amount of money for the effort and investment. Plus, if you picked up some from along the roadside, you had the pleasure of knowing you made your community better looking.

Even "junking" a car for scrap doesn't bring the money you would think it should. If you're looking for a way to earn money fast, this should not be first on anyone's list.

Make a fortune with a metal detector?

The next make-fast-money scheme is just that, much more a scheme than any type of opportunity. I hesitate to even mention it, but some of the arguments for it being a lucrative activity are rather persuasive.

That's investing in a metal detector and hit the beach. You'll be combining two wonderful activities enjoying the beach and the ocean or lake and earning a great income.

While you will enjoy your walk it's far less likely that you'll make enough money on your finds to buy an order of boardwalk fries. I'm not sure where this scheme first started, but it's really not worth your time or energy. And certainly isn't your path to leaving the rat race behind you.

Then there's the promise of being able to work at home and make an amazing income. These advertisements have you wondering why you're even slaving away in the rat race. As your parents or somebody has probably warned you in the past, "If it sounds too good to be true, it .probably is."

That's what these work-at-home schemes are, nothing but schemes that promise everything, but delivery nothing. While there are any numbers of different methods that suggest you can make a great income working from home, there is one scheme that has been around forever. Yes, even before the internet days.

Stuffing envelopes

That's the promise of making money stuffing envelopes or assembling crafts in the privacy of your home

The catch?

You have to buy the needed supplies from the advertiser. And even that wouldn't be so bad, but then the "employer" tells you he can't pay you because your work doesn't meet his high standards. And of course, he won't even reimburse you for the cost of supplies. That's a "lose-lose" situation for you if there ever was one.

Testing video games online

Laugh if you want but this was once a great way of making money. For a time, it appeared to be quite lucrative If you loved video games, imagine how it must have felt to sit in front of the screen playing an awesome game.

And the only words ringing in your ears are your parents who always told you that you were wasting your time, there's no way to make money playing video games. For example, in one of the later chapters, you'll meet a young man who is making a great income playing video games online.

Not only that but there were also several other ways to make money through your vast knowledge of certain video games. For example, many earned a great income by creating items from the games, then selling these to gamers. Unfortunately, that market has been eaten up by larger manufacturers, who have finally realized how popular the right video game can be.

So what's left?

This list of how-not-to-boost your income wasn't meant to discourage you to step outside the rate race beltway. It wasn't meant to pour water on your dream of financial income.

But it is a warning that you should be careful when looking for a side income. There is still one method that in the last twenty or so years has remained a constant money-maker requiring the least amount of startup funds is an online income.

And with the maturity and the blossoming of various niches on the web today, more ways exist than ever before to earn what's called a passive income or even multiple streams of income, to get you to your final goal.

In the next chapter, we delve into the topic a bit deeper to help steer you in the right direction – a passive income that not only brings in the needed extra money, but one that comes close to matching your own interests and talents.

CHAPTER 6:

~

Why an Online Business?

So why would you even consider starting an online business?

Because, despite what anyone says, it's still one of the most inexpensive ways to start a business and earn that extra income required in order to walk away from the rat race.

In fact, depending on the way you choose to present yourself on the web, it may cost nothing – and you'll be able to create a nominal income much quicker than most people think is possible.

For dollar-for-dollar, there's nothing that beats your return on investment like a web-based business.

If we were talking about only money, that would be an overwhelming advantage, but let's throw in the opportunity about doing what you love – or at the very least spreading the love of your hobby or interest to others. They may discover they too have a passion for it.

So what do you need to get started?

Think about it. You don't need to even invest in a desk to work at if you don't want to. You can use your current home office. Or, you can decide not to use your home office.

What happens when you want to go on vacation?

You go! Of course, you'll want to keep an eye on your business while you're gone. The hotel you're staying at can accommodate you in many ways. You can do a few minutes or even an hour of work from the lobby of the hotel in the many offices they have for traveling business executives or the privacy of your hotel room. When you're done, simply dip yourself in the pool or begin your day of sightseeing.

The real advantage of this is that when you return home, you're not facing a week's worth of duties you neglected and have to get caught up with. You're still current with your business. It doesn't get much better than this.

This is the nearly perfect way to keep your "day job," and raise your income to put toward lowering your expenses. It is in fact, another one of those 'win-win' choices we've talked about.

Your next step in deciding your ideal online business is to take stock of the topics you're most interested in. For some individuals, this will be easy. Let's say you love to write. You want to escape the rat race so you can finish those novels filed away in your computer. You'll want to start with anything and everything that deals with books.

Perhaps you love to cook and would like to share recipes with others, this would make a great a great website, powered by the many ways you can earn money online. You may even want to write a recipe e-book or a "yes you can cook" for those who want to learn.

And all the hobbies are represented on the web. Love a certain breed of dog? You can start an online business catering to doggy supplies while blogging about different breeds of dogs.

So you've taken account of your interests and fitting them into an online business. You've narrowed your choice down to a select few which have what's called a profitable niche market. This is a specialized market that usually comes under the umbrella of larger markets.

Because the internet attracts such a potentially large customer base, you can drill down and target people in niche markets that are far too small for a neighborhood retail shop or even a shop in a larger city.

Here's a silly example. If you've ever watched the Simpsons, there's one episode where their neighbor Ned Flanders opens a "left-handed" store at the local mall. It doesn't bring in the traffic he thought it would. About ten percent of the population is left-handed, but that doesn't represent a market that could sustain a large enough traffic flow even in a large neighborhood.

But it could very well work as the premise of an online internet enterprise. All you need to do Google left-handed stores to see how many websites and virtual stores there are.

If you're having problems choosing a good online venture, check out the few examples below to give you ideas. Once you get thinking along these lines, you might find an idea that sparks your creativity, or you may brainstorm to something that suits your personality and your preferences better.

Before we jump in there, I'd like to let you in on a secret the most successful online businesspersons use. They employ a technique called "multiple streams of income." It really is nicely and forthrightly named. That means you don't depend on just one site or one blog bringing in the big bucks.

Let's use that example of the left-handed store again. Let's decide, in fact, that you're going to start a website that sells theses left-handed products. But, you decide, either as a backup plan or more likely than not to boost your second income, to start a second site or blog and sell in another or similar niche.

Now, with this in mind, let's see what kinds of ways, you can create multiple streams of income.

Affiliate Marketing

The granddaddy of all the money-generating techniques found on the web, affiliate marketing is still a tough method to improve on. The only stumbling block you may discover is that just one affiliation may not bring in the cash you're looking for on a regular basis.

In a nutshell, here's how it works. You choose a company of which to be an affiliate. You'll find that many online entrepreneurs choose to be an amazon.com affiliate, just because of the extended reach of all their amazing variety of products on their site.

Amazon, we might as well continue with this example, will then assign you a link for your customers to use to take them to the Amazon site and make a transaction. You get a certain percentage of the sales. As long as that link is used to buy the product.

Let's say, for example, you really love the idea of the left-handed store. When you become an affiliate of Amazon and you recommend a new left-handed product through the Amazon link and your customer makes a purchase . . poof . . . you make a percentage of the price of that product.

The advantage of this is that you won't get bogged down with fulfilling orders.

Who, me? Blog

Yes, you can blog, especially if you have an area of expertise. And yes, you are fast becoming an expert on left-handed products, information, and history. Establish yourself as an authority on the topic simply by reading up on it. You'll find your income increasing with time.

But, keep in mind, you can blog about any other topics as well. These days just about every business or expert has a blog, so you need to either be passionate about your topic or to pick something that piques the interests of the ordinary person. Hopefully, you can choose a topic on which you are an expert and is also a popular topic.

What's involved?

While you may like the idea of blogging, you may have wondered what was involved to garner enough traffic to keep your enthusiasm for it. It's actually easier than you think.

First, think about providing your readers and potential readers with content they can use – and do it in an entertaining way. For example, if you write, then talk about some strategies you use that others may not know about. Ask for reader interaction and then be sure to comment on all the responses you receive from readers.

Secondly, you want to be yourself. Today more than ever readers want to know more about you. It helps to generate a sense of loyalty for starters. Don't be afraid to write what you think. It's better than being "wishy-washy" and not coming down on one side or the other.

A stimulating discussion is healthy. Just don't let it degenerate into name-calling or bigoted roads.

If you're going to start a blog then be sure to carry through with it and write on a regular basis. It doesn't need to be every day. In fact, that seems a bit overwhelming not only for you but for the reader as well. Two or three times a week is the perfect goal, especially if it's quality content.

How do you earn money blogging?

First, depending on the topic, you may find some great affiliate marketing programs that offer tremendous e-products that you could sell, including e-books. But, you should also check out the variety of advertising options available, from click ads to blogging networks. You'd be surprised at how the activity of blogging has created its own lucrative niche on the internet.

And the best aspect yet, is that you can start a blog in less than an hour and unlike a website, you can get a blog site for free.

CHAPTER 7:

~

One Size Cannot Fit All

It's amazing, really.

There are as many paths to financial people as there are people who desire it intensely enough. If you're looking for a technical manual that tells you step-by-step the sure-fire way to make enough money to live on, you're going to be disappointed.

It not like putting the exercise bicycle together. Step 1, place this part into this part and tighten the bolt.

If that were the case, then the rat race would be much less crowded. Others certainly can set you in the right direction and those who have traveled this road successfully can tell you what worked for them. But ultimately you and you alone have to travel the road to discover your shortest, quickest and most satisfying way to your own interpretation of financial freedom.

To show you exactly what I mean, I've profiled five different people who took the plunge and dropped out of the rat race. Each did it in his or her own way. Not every one of these five individuals succeeded. But the point is that each took their own route.

Alex – Video game player

Alex is 21 and a high school dropout. He didn't see the use of sitting in class any longer than was necessary. So he walked away from school in his senior year. Because of that choice, the best job he could get was working in a warehouse, earning $2500 a month. And he knew that he was lucky to get that. He lived with his parents which kept his expenses to a minimum. In fact, they were only $1,100 a month – less than half of what he made monthly.

Alex found himself dissatisfied with his job at the warehouse. It was, surprisingly, a lot like the rat race of high school from which he walked away from. "They" the management, that is, controlled your steps from six in the morning to three in the afternoon. He found the two places eerily similar – his job in the warehouse and high school. In both he had a set time, not to mention limited, time to eat. Set times to take his breaks and yes, there really was a regime of rules some which were pure nonsense, just like he encountered in high school.

After work nearly daily, he would then get to what he loved doing, playing video games. He would stream onto the website twitch.com, a live streaming video platform where he built a large following and became quite an attraction. People loved to watch him play, they said, because they could feel his pure passion for the game.

He did this for two years despite some people criticizing that he should grow up and consider his future. Eventually, he followed their advice, but not in the manner anyone in the rat race had expected. He quitted his "day job" at the warehouse and is now thriving, financially secure, doing exactly what he loves.

As you can see it would be most difficult for all of us to replicate the exact process, but, we can apply that pattern of breaking through to financial freedom to our own personal circumstances.

Meet Bonnie

Bonnie Baker is a 28-year old software engineer, making $90,000 a year. After spending all that time in college and now working fulltime, she realizes she doesn't like her job. It doesn't fulfill her. In fact, what she dislikes most about her job is that no one around her smiles much. They always seem to be grumpy. But more than that they lack a sense of humor. Now, that's one character trait Bonnie has. In fact, laughter has seen her through her most stressful days at work.

In the three years, she has been doing this type of work, she's been able to save $200,000. She took her savings and invested it in high-dividend stocks, which gave her about $1,300 a month on which to live.

Bonnie then decided to decrease the hours she worked at her engineering job to part-time and transitioned herself onto working on the internet, creating humorous videos on Youtube.

She's far less stressed working this way and realized that she's half-way home to financial freedom. But even this much has lowered the stress on her. Bonnie knows that she's not even going to need the part-time software engineering job much longer.

Carl Spenser – Then and Now

Carl Spenser has been considering leaving the rat race for some time. He's already working on decreasing his expenses. How serious is he? He has two roommates to help lower the expenses of rent utilities and even groceries.

Because of his wonderful roommates, his total month-ly expenses are only $600 of which half goes toward rent. He doesn't own a car and instead commutes to work on his bicycle.

His "rat race" job, as he calls it is, going into a vita-min and herbal supplement store four days a week a sales associate and cashier. Carl is the first to admit that it isn't that stressful. And he makes sure everyone knows, he's not out to climb the corporate ladder of this franchise.

The one advantage, which he tries to downplay, is the fact that when the store has no customers, he works on his blog – a how-to blog on getting 6-pack abs.

Once he's home at night, he doesn't spend his time watching television or net flicks or anything else for that matter. Instead, he spends about three hours managing his blog, videos, and email lists. He also promotes other fitness products.

It's during this three-hour block that he gets into the "zone" as he calls it, enjoying every moment of what he's doing.

It took Carl approximately a year and a half, he's making an astounding $80,000 from his business. And now has finally moved into a place that he loves.

Where will you be in the next year and a half?

Then there is Darren

Among all of our examples, it's no wonder that Darren Hamilton is the most frustrated and most stuck in his place in the rate race.

Darren has been in his job as a barista at a local coffee shop for eight years. The job is relatively easy and the first few years were even fun. He enjoyed making different types of coffee. But what Darren especially like was meeting all the people, talking to them and getting to know them. He knew his regular customers by their first names and they appreciated that.

His customers, in return, made sure they called him by name and tipped him well. But after eight years, he felt trapped. The whole barista thing wasn't as exciting or even interesting as it was when he first began.

He'd like nothing better than to quit, especially on those days when the manager or owner or someone shot off their mouth and started complaining. Oh yeah, he's at the point in his life where he'd love to quit and find another job. But, that was the kicker. He was fearful of what would happen if he went with his instincts, walked out the door one day and never came back. He was afraid he couldn't find another job.

Compounding his problems is that he's beginning to see more signs of depression. He knows it's because of the unnecessary stress he's under at work.

The truth is that he's making a decent sum of money but he hates to spend it.

Every time he spends money, it only reminds him of working.

Darren is 36 years old, takes medication for depression and seems to spend most of his free time lamenting that he never got out of his comfort zone..

He'd like nothing better but to start over – but then the fear creeps in.

How much of yourself do you see in Darren?

Edie loves the lifestyle

It's true. Edie loves the lifestyle she's living. She's a regional marketing manager with a dot-com company and sure she's set to be next in line for the position of vice president of marketing when the current vice president retires in about a year and a half.

Until then she's staying right where she is. She makes $120,000 a year. But she's loaded with debt. Why? Because she's always spending more money than what she is earning. She has the most expensive tastes when it comes to clothes, handbags, and shoes.

Oh, she'll tell everybody that she always buying these because it's all part of the appearance of looking like a successful manager. She tells her closest friends, if she dresses the part, the easier it is to gain others' respect. While there is some truth to that, Edie merely uses it as an excuse to go on a shopping spree once a month or so.

The truth, which she lets no one know, is that she hates her job even though she loves the pay. Even if she wasn't in a high-level position within the firm, she'd still be overspending, including eating out at all the overpriced restaurants she's grown accustomed to.

Then one day it happened. No, not the promotion, but declaring bankruptcy. She could only spend more than she made for so long. She finally got her charge cards so maxed out that she couldn't juggle the payments any longer.

Now she's still working in a job she hates, but with a bankruptcy on her credit report.

Passive streams of income

As you can see from these illustrations, many individuals have found financial freedom, while keeping their options open, you might say. What they did was simply what all internet entrepreneurs would advise you. Find passive streams of income. If you can do this, then you can be present at your day job while your internet business kept itself busy working on your behave.

The difference between being a rat racer and an entrepreneur can be identified at least one way: needing to be in a physical location to get paid, much like our friend Darren. When you start working on the internet, it's open for business twenty-four hours seven- days a week and doesn't demand your presence in order for you to receive an income.

Nobody says that you'll be rolling in the dough after a year and a half like Carl, but then, not everyone gave most of their spare time to their desire either like this person did. Many individuals wait until they're up against a wall, whatever they deem that to be. It's only then that they think about accumulating more money in order to walk away from the rat race.

What about the nagging fear?

It depends on which fear you're talking about. Is it the fear of leaving your current position and not finding financial freedom? Is it the fear and humiliation that you might return to a boring nine-to-five day job?

Or is it the fear of being wildly successful while stepping outside of your comfort zone.

The truth of the matter is that living a financially secure life that is based on fear, is, without a doubt, the most powerful pull back into the rat race – or preventing you from even trying.

One of the things you need to do on your way to financial freedom, other than never quit, is to refine your perspective on the idea of failure. Too many of us fear failure that may come at the end. Some folks simply believe that since you tried once or even twice that the dream you hold, your yearning for financial freedom isn't part of your destiny. You aren't one of the "lucky" ones to gain that path to financial freedom.

Instead, you need to view one misstep, one stumble on the liberating road out of the rat race as a learning lesson. It's a way to say okay, this wasn't the right choice, at least the timing was wrong. But I have so many more options up my sleeve I know one of them will work.

And if none of those works, you continue assuring yourself, something even better will be coming your way. But mark my words, you say more options up my sleeve I know one of them will work.

Keep in mind that when you make your first, tentative step to an online business, there is no pressure that you have to create the "next big thing," the one business that keeps the internet abuzz. Our online business people from this chapter who succeeded had modest ideas and still end up making more money with less hassle than they experienced at their "day jobs."

The other advantage of an online business is that because of the low or no cost, you can actually start up more than one. Don't rush and do this all at once though. See how your first is working out. If you seem to have found your place, then create another one – you can even take an entirely different business.

Regardless of the number of examples of those who remained in the rat race and those who broke free, the final decision is yours.

CHAPTER 8:

~

Be Resourceful and Taking Responsibility for Your Life

You've already noticed that every person with the desire to leave the rat race and the yearning to be financially free, doesn't always succeed. In fact, if the truth is known, there are probably more people who failed once, gave up, and filed back in line into the rat race.

The trouble with that approach, though, that individual will never know if he could have made it, because he didn't give himself a fair chance. Instead of analyzing where he went wrong, what mistakes he made, and reviewing his strengths and his weaknesses, he simply set out blaming everybody and everything for what he calls, "his bad luck."

Soon his bad luck has turned into his destiny. "It was in my stars," he'll tell you, not to be one of those very lucky people who get all the breaks and just waltzed into a life of financial freedom effortlessly.

And as you prepare to leave the rat race, he's the one arguing the loudest and most vehemently that you will never make it. "It's a jungle out there," he'll warn you. In other words, he'll do everything within his power to keep you from even trying by relating all the worst details of his attempt.

Instead of taking responsibility for their failure so they can give it a second try, they instead prefer to play "the blame game." They would rather point fingers at the circumstances and even others around them for their return to the rat race.

Many psychologists call this the "victim mentality." The fact of the matter is that taking responsibility for your own actions – for your own destiny doesn't come easily to many people.

Many individuals will do this basically for one reason: it makes them feel better. It soothes the open wound they have that tells them daily they weren't good enough. We all have a small voice that tries to tell us we're not good enough for one thing or another. These individuals not only listen to it until it becomes a big voice and then actually believe what that voice is saying.

If you dig below the surface of their criticism of your desire, you'll probably find some limiting belief they've developed to comfort them. And to keep themselves in this comfort zone, you need to adhere to their limiting beliefs.

Don't allow them to make their opinions part of your limiting beliefs.

We've already taken a good look at five individuals who all from different walks of life. Each of them yearned for a profitable online business. As you saw, though, not all of them succeeded.

What characteristics do you need to be a financial success as an entrepreneur? I'll give you a hint. While expertise in finance and the business you're about to enter is vital, you can always learn that while you're on the job. What you really need are three simple, but powerful traits:

1. Take responsibility

Before you claim that you already do take responsibility and you very well might remember that you're leaving the rat race, it will mean that more responsibility will now be on your shoulders. If you're used to blaming others for either job losses, late presentations or even not being promoted, you're in for a loud wake-up call when you step out of the race.

There won't be anybody but yourself to take the blame. And even if there were, it's still your business. So, what am I talking about when I say take responsibility? Let me give you a vivid example of what mean.

Let's say you made a judgment call and it didn't work out. Let's even say you lost a good deal of money in the process. Are you going to pack up and head back toward the rat race, blaming anything from the economic conditions at the time of the decision to your competitor or even perhaps one of your employees if you've hired any yet?

In reality, it's your business, your golden ticket to your financial freedom and your chance to leave the rat race. Don't start playing the blame game. If you do this, it'll feel as if you're throwing away control of your future and allowing those activities and even people outside of you to control your destiny. And you know that you're the only person that can write his or her destiny.

There are plenty of people ready to point their fingers at someone else the moment a business starts to falter. Even in the workplace, you'll meet more people than you can imagine who will point the finger the moment something goes wrong

I'd like to use the actions a Harry Truman for a moment as a perfect example of how to take the responsibility for his actions, even if afterward, it appeared to be a wrong decision.

As you well know, Truman assumed the presidency of the United States upon the sudden death of Franklin D. Roosevelt. The country was in the midst of World War II. Roosevelt, it seems, didn't keep Truman in the loop about the state of the war and related scientific developments toward the building of an atomic bomb.

When presented with all the facts, Truman chose to drop not just one but two on Japan. The war ended shortly thereafter.

But not before Truman, as you can imagine from today's perspective took a lot of heat for his decision. And even if he had misgivings about the decision, he stood by and took responsibility for his actions. He didn't blame his advisors or anybody else. He and he alone made the final decision, he told the press.

That's wasn't atypical of Truman either. He had a plague on his desk in the Oval Office which simply said, "The buck stops here." This means that while people were busy pointing fingers at each other and playing the blame game, he took full responsibility for anything and everything that happened during his presidency.

When you start your trek to financial freedom, Truman wouldn't be a bad example to bring to your memory every now and then.

Besides, if you really think about it you're wasting time blaming others when you could be using that valuable time into finding solutions that will repair the problem. The longer you allow the mistake or misjudgment to linger uncorrected the potentially larger the problem grows.

There's never a shortage of excuses

Very often individuals who have tried and failed at an online business or stumbled along the path to eventual financial freedom have a host of excuses. "I didn't have the time to give the business the attention it deserved." "I didn't know enough about running a business."

It could be that they were just stuck with a whole of "lack." What do I mean by this? They'll tell you they lacked the money, the support or they didn't have the right personnel under them.

What they're trying to say is that they didn't have the necessary resources to continue. While this may be what their ego is telling them, in reality, there really isn't ever a lack of resources floating around you or on the internet. What they don't realize is that they lacked the *resourcefulness* to continue. There's a large difference in those two words.

Many of us at one time have lacked the proper resources for one career or activity or another. That, though, never stopped them. They employed their resourcefulness to discover a way to get what they needed.

This stands in stark contrast to others who claim they could easily become a bestselling author but were never given the chance of going to college. If you scratch the surface, what you find under those words is the sentiment that is merely an excuse.

They could have just sat down and started writing to see how it turned out. Then they could have moved on from there. Many brilliant writers never went to college or if they did go eventually dropped out. They are just putting a wall of excuses between their Big Dream and reality as they see it. They aren't taking responsibility for their own actions – or lack of action.

Instead, those who have exited the rat race, not returned have found the exhilarating freedom to make their own choices without the limiting fear of always asking, "How much will that cost? *Your choices in life reflect your resourcefulness.* You may not believe you have any, but you'd be amazed when pushed, what you find within yourself.

What exactly is resourcefulness?

It's the ability to rise above the challenges the world throws at you by developing a different perspective on the problem. For starters, "problems" are for these individuals, nothing more than challenges and even opportunities to discover creative alternatives to your present condition.

The bottom line is that it consists of using the resources you have at hand, using the skills you're good at to creatively overcome the challenge.

Those with a resourcefulness mentality are usually those who don't label their current situation as a problem. Instead, they call it a challenge or even an opportunity. It's an opportunity, they'll tell you, to discover a new and exciting way of doing something or of looking at their circumstances differently.

What they don't do is blame others, to blame circumstance or anything or anybody else for what they're facing at the moment. They are creatively and eagerly doing more work with fewer resources.

Conclusion

It takes a special kind of person to walk away from the rat race and begin his own journey toward financial freedom.

Everyone who tries this, no doubt, has special reasons all his own for doing so. Some are tired of their boss, others are yearning for more time to participate in what they love doing and still, others are just plain fed with the material consumerism that shouts at us from every corner of society.

No doubt you have your own reasons for ditching the tiring and seemingly endless race that gains you neither kudos nor respect. But, before you even begin your journey you need to ensure you want this lifestyle with the intensity that you'll have to ignore the naysayers and continue seeking your freedom.

This also means that even before you take one step toward accumulating your nest egg, you need to know where you stand right now financially. If you don't know where you are now, how can you ever hope to get to where you want to be?

You need to see how much money you're making at the moment and then check how expenses line up with your income. Then, and only then, can you decide where your current level of spending is taking you?

After you do that, you need to take charge of what your expenses look like, looking especially at your largest payments first. For some it's a house payment, for others it's a car payment or, for you it may be student loans.

As scary an activity as this is for some of us, it *is* necessary. Once that's done, then you can check out how to either increase your income or decrease your spending. Better yet, you should seriously consider doing both.

To know how to get where you are now to where you want to be one of the things you'll need to do is to review your strengths and weaknesses. Seriously think about what you love doing, what you'd rather not do and then line your search for a second income up with these.

Chances are one of the reasons you're looking for a way out of the rat race right now is because you find your current job or career is not providing the satisfaction you want from it. You may resent the time you "invest" in your job because it's taking time away from your family or from working on your Big Dream.

Only you can decide that and only you can make the decision to start a side income to get you through the rat race and to financial freedom.

It's not necessarily something everyone has the ability to do, but for those who persist the rewards are sweet. Nothing less than all the time you care to devote -- and money to go along with it – to do literally anything you desire. Or nothing at all.

As you travel your journey to freedom from a dependency on a regular paycheck, you may want to think about a few of the ideas and tips below.

Gaining your financial freedom does not happen overnight.

But it will happen. You must promise yourself that. You must also be kind to yourself along with your journey. For example, give yourself permission to take as much time as you need to get there. Remember, this is not the rat race anymore. Achieving financial freedom also takes a daily focus on your next step. And more than anything else, remain committed to the cause. You know exactly why you're doing it.

You'll discover as you start your steps to your Big Dream that the perfect person with the perfect piece of information or knowledge that you need just seems to pop up. If you find this happening to you, then you're experiencing what many individuals have called synchronicity.

It's something akin to the universe nudging you, letting you know you're on the right path. This should encourage you and give you the desire to work, even more, put in another hour of work on your Big Dream. Or as if by magic, you'll find that you're talking with precisely the right person who can help you, or seminars that answers some of the questions you've been asking lately.

There's no question about it. When you start your financial road to freedom, there will be many stops along the way, where you wonder if you're doing the right thing. You'll wonder some nights that perhaps staying in the race and just skating by and accepting a paycheck – however meager it may seem – wasn't all that bad after all. But when all is said and done, you realize you the path to financial freedom is the only road for you;

One last word

It may seem ironic or it may seem Zen-like. Whatever you call it, more than one person has remarked on this most amazing turn of events, once they get to the point of basking the freedom from a regular paycheck. You discover that instead of working on your business because you need the money, you work because . . . well, you want to. You work not with the purpose of generating more money, but with the purpose of enjoying yourself.

That's because your motivation has changed dramatically. When you were in the rat race, work meant survival. It meant that paycheck that would give you one more week of income to put towards the necessities of your lifestyle. You had a "need" to work.

Now that you're working for your benefit, to advance the bottom line you want to work. And the difference between the two words, "need" and "want" is remark-able. It's perhaps the difference between fear and love: The fear of not being able to survive without a pay-check, compared to the love of doing what you want to do, no matter whether you're paid or not.

At the start of your journey, you may have assumed that your actions were clearly motivated by money. As you get closer to your goals, you'll feel your thinking subtly changing. The money, sure, is nice. But what you've gained by all this activity and commitment is an accumulation of real wealth. There's no way you can measure wealth in dollars and cents alone.

That's because real wealth is about gathering a variety of enriching experiences. It's not about the money in the bank, but rather how the money allows you to en-joy the world on your terms, doing whatever it is that you find you truly love.

Thank you for reading "Make Money Work For You". If you enjoyed this book. Please take some time to share your thoughts and post a review. It'd be greatly appreciated.

I wish you the best and good luck!

Bruce Walker

www.ingramcontent.com/pod-product-compliance
Lightning Source LLC
Chambersburg PA
CBHW031905200326
41597CB00012B/543